BABAR
RETURNS
Adapted by
Lesley Young

It was night in Celesteville and the whole palace was in darkness, except for the kitchen. Light was streaming from the open fridge as Flora rummaged through the shelves. "Mangoes, tangerines, bananas, marzipan on toast..."

"That's the kind of midnight snack that will give you nightmares," said a deep voice behind her. "Why are you up so late?"

"It's the tennis match tomorrow," said Flora. "I'm so worried about it I can't sleep. You see, I'm always missing shots and Alexander gets furious with me."

"Perhaps you should stop thinking about your weaknesses and find out if your opponents have any," said Babar.

Flora looked puzzled. "Can you explain?"

Babar put a pile of food on the table and settled down. As he spread butter on the bread, Babar began, "A long time ago..."

It was a busy day in the city and Babar was watching the people from the balcony of the Old Lady's house. Although the sun was shining, and all the birds were singing, Babar looked sad and his trunk drooped.

The Old Lady joined him on the balcony. "Good morning, Babar. What a lovely day!"

"I suppose it is," sighed Babar.

"Does the sunshine make you sad?" asked the Old Lady, kindly.

"I was just thinking about…" Babar began, looking at the trees.

The Old Lady understood. "I know - Celeste, Arthur and Cornelius. Cheer up - let's go for a walk."

Babar was looking through his binoculars as he and the Old Lady walked along. Suddenly, he put them down and rubbed his eyes.

"What is it, Babar?" asked the Old Lady.

"Nothing," said Babar. " I'm imagining things."

But then he heard, "Babar! Babar!" There were Celeste and Arthur looking at him from behind the bushes. He stood up as they ran towards him, crying.

"Is it really you? How did you get here?" asked Babar.

"When you didn't return we came to look for you," said Celeste.

"But we got lost!" said Arthur. "I knew we'd find you if we got lost enough… I'm hungry," he added.

"Then I know just the place to take you," said the Old Lady. She took them to a cake shop that sold plump cream puffs.

"There's nothing like this in the jungle," said Arthur, happily.

"Now we must do some shopping," said the Old Lady. She took them to a clothes shop where Arthur found a smart sailor suit and Celeste chose a pink dress.

In a perfume shop the Old Lady chose some dusting powder and a scent spray for Celeste.

"Now for music!" cried the Old Lady, leading the way into a music shop where she bought them a fine gramophone and some records.

"We mustn't forget fun!" said the Old Lady, and off they went to a toy shop where they were all kitted out with roller skates.

"Thank you!" they all cried.

Back in her parlour the Old Lady poured tea. "We came to bring you back home, Babar," said Celeste. "We all need you."

Arthur helped himself to another cream puff. "It's terrible. The hunter is chasing us deeper and deeper into the jungle."

The hunter! Babar turned icy cold at the words. It was the hunter who had shot his mother, leaving Babar to fend for himself.

"You must go - they need your help," said the Old Lady.

"I know," agreed Babar. Together they packed up all their presents into the little red car. "I am going to miss you," said the Old Lady.

"Thank you for everything," said Babar. Then the car sped off, with the Old Lady waving and Babar calling, "I'll come back one day!"

Soon they were travelling over mountains and across bridges until Babar could see the jungle in the distance, throbbing under a cloud of heat. "It's good to be back," he said.

"We're not there yet," said Celeste. "We go down there." She pointed down a damp track to a dark and gloomy clearing.

"But that's the darkest, most miserable part of the whole jungle," said Babar.

As they stared unhappily into the dark, they heard a noise…

The bushes round about them were shaking as if they were alive. Celeste and Arthur huddled close to Babar as he pulled out his walking stick and lashed at the bushes.

"Hey! Careful there!" Three pairs of tusks emerged, joined to Pompadour, Cornelius, and Celeste and Arthur's mother who hurried to hug her children.

"How are you, Pompadour?" asked Babar.

"Lucky to be alive, all things considered," rumbled the elephant. "But what's happened to you? You're as green as creepers!"

"This is just a suit," said Babar. "It can come off, you know." He took off his jacket.

"My tusks!" boomed Cornelius. "You can shed your skin - just like a snake!"

"I'm glad I've found you all safe and sound," said Babar.

"You're lucky you found us at all," said Pompadour.

"We kept moving," explained Cornelius, "thinking we would find a really safe place, but now we realise there is no such thing."

"No - not even this miserable place," said the old King, who was coming out of the bushes. He looked older than ever.

Suddenly there was a roar, and the sound of something heavy crashing through the undergrowth. "It's the hunter!" cried Pompadour. "Run!"

The elephants tore off in all directions. "Hurry, run, Babar!" trumpeted Cornelius.

Babar jumped into his car and tried desperately to start the engine. Nothing happened. Behind him he could hear the hunter's jeep coming nearer. Suddenly the car leapt forward and Babar drove off as fast as he could into the jungle.

That night the elephants gathered to make plans. The King stood on a mound of earth and boomed, "We will run no further. Tomorrow we will drive the hunter away. I call for an elephant stampede!"

Babar stepped forward and said, "Your Highness, this is madness. The hunter has a gun - we must beat him by using our wits."

"You have been away too long," said Cornelius, softly. "You have forgotten what jungle-life is like."

"Has Babar forgotten, too, that the stampede is a great elephant tradition?" said the King. "I have spoken. It will be done!"

Next morning Babar and Celeste watched the sunrise. "Tell me again about the opera," said Celeste.

"I think that's what put Arthur to sleep at last!" said Babar.

"If the hunter catches us, we'll see it all from inside..." Celeste began.

"Cages," shuddered Babar. "Not if I can help it."

At the same time, all the other elephants were forming a long line. They were led by the King, and each animal gripped the tail of the one in front.

One elephant just watched the procession. He was too old to join the stampede. Then the line disappeared into the distance with the elephants' war chant fading as it went.

Suddenly Babar, Celeste and Arthur burst into the clearing. Babar was in a panic. "Quick - where are the others?" he asked the old elephant, breathlessly.

"They've left for the stampede, of course," he answered.

"Come on," said Babar to Celeste and Arthur. "They can't have gone far. We can catch up with them."

"You won't be able to stop them," the old elephant called after them.

But Babar and the others were too late. At the hunter's camp, all the elephants were locked inside a corral he had built from logs. The hunter walked around it, slapping his leg with his riding crop and laughing loudly with an evil laugh.

The King turned to Cornelius, "What is this ivory he speaks of?"

"I believe, Your Majesty, he is talking about our tusks," replied Cornelius. "I've heard they are worth quite a fortune when they sell them in the big cities."

"How horrible," shuddered the King, sending ripples down his folds of grey skin. "I have failed my people. I should have listened to Babar - he knew that the hunter would trick us into this trap."

The elephants stared sadly out of the corral, not knowing what was going to happen next.

Babar parted the bushes and looked across to the corral. "We're too late," he groaned. "The hunter has trapped everyone."

"It's all over," moaned Celeste.

"No it's not," said Babar. He stretched out his trunk and whispered to the others.

A few minutes later the hunter heard war-like music echoing through the jungle. He grabbed his gun and rushed off to see where it was coming from.

Babar watched him hurry past. "Now!" he whispered to the others. They rushed to the corral and heaved at the gate. The trapped elephants pushed from inside.

At last the gate gave way and the elephants poured out. "Go to the river!" cried Babar.

Then the hunter found the hidden gramophone that the Old Lady had bought Babar, and realised he'd been tricked…

The hunter came back into the clearing just in time to see the last of the elephants streaming into the jungle. He raised his rifle and prepared to fire.

At that moment Babar appeared, holding Celeste's perfume spray. He squirted it right into the evil hunter's eyes. The hunter cried and staggered backwards.

Babar raced through the jungle after the others. At the river's edge he turned and waited for the hunter, standing at the edge of a wide log. The hunter climbed on to the log and aimed his rifle at Babar. Babar yelled, "Now, Arthur!"

Arthur pulled a vine attached to a piece of wood wedged in front of the log. As it came out, it freed the roller skates that Babar had tied to the log. The log zoomed down the bank carrying the hunter towards the river where crocodiles were swimming hungrily.

"Hooray!" shouted the elephants. But their joy was short-lived. Next morning they found the old king lying beside a patch of strange-looking mushrooms. His skin looked odd and shrivelled.

"What is it?" asked Babar, as one of the mushrooms fell out of the King's mouth.

"These mushrooms must be poisonous," said Cornelius, as the King rolled over. A hush fell over the jungle. The king was dead.

"This is a dreadful place," cried Babar. "We must leave here and never return."

So the elephants formed a sad line and walked until they reached their old home.

The grass was bright, and the air was clean and fresh. The elephants trumpeted happily. Some splashed in the river, while others shook fruit off the trees.

"It's so good to be home," sighed Celeste.

Pompadour called for attention. "It is now our duty to appoint a new king. There is only one among us who has the wisdom and the vision to lead us."

Cornelius stepped forward. "Well, thank you for the compliment," he said, "but I'm afraid I cannot accept. Babar is the one who must be king."

Pompadour snorted crossly - he had been about to choose Babar himself!

"Long live King Babar!" trumpeted the whole herd of elephants.

Babar knelt as Cornelius placed the crown on his head. Then he stood up and called for silence.

"The days of running and hiding, and living in fear are over. The jungle is changing all around us, and we must learn to change with it. I promise that together we will grow strong and happy."

The elephants trumpeted a happy salute.

"And that," said Babar to Flora, "is how we defeated the evil hunter. We were able to do it because we knew his weaknesses. Of course," he added, "we were lucky too!"

"We thought we heard voices!" Celeste, Alexander and Pom appeared round the door.

"It's a good thing I made this a family-size sandwich," said Babar.

Flora turned to Alexander. "Have you ever noticed that Pom has a weak backhand?"

"As a matter of fact I have," said Alexander, grinning.

"I'm so excited I can't sleep," cried Flora. "I think we might win the tennis match!"

At last the three children went back to bed. "Suddenly I'm hungry," said Celeste. "Could I have one of your special sandwiches?"

"Of course," smiled Babar, "if you've got time. I can't leave out the most important ingredient - a good story!"

Based on the animated series
"Babar"
a Nelvana-Ellipse Presentation,
a Nelvana Production in Association
with The Clifford Ross Company.

Based on characters created by
Jean and Laurent de Brunhoff.

Carnival
An imprint of the Children's Division
of the Collins Publishing Group
8 Grafton Street, London W1X 3LA

Published by Carnival 1990

ISBN 0 00 193224 1

Printed in Great Britain by
BPCC Paulton Books Limited

This book is set in New Century Schoolbook 14 point